Action Sports Library

JET SKIING

Bob Italia

Published by Abdo & Daughters, 6535 Cecilia Circle, Edina, Minnesota 55439.

Library bound edition distributed by Rockbottom Books, Pentagon Tower, P.O. Box 36036, Minneapolis, Minnesota 55435.

Printed in the United States.

ISBN:1-56239-075-9

Library of Congress Card Catalog Number: 91-073022

Cover Photos: ALLSPORT USA / PHOTOGRAPHER, 1991.
Inside Photos: ALLSPORT USA / PHOTOGRAPHER, 1991.

Warning: The series *Action Sports Library* is intended as entertainment for children. These sporting activities should never be attempted without the proper conditioning, training, instruction, supervision, and equipment.

Edited by Rosemary Wallner

CONTENTS

A jet ski may look like a toy—
but it's really a boat!

JET SKIING

What's a Jet Ski?

A jet ski is a small, maneuverable personal water-craft that is powered by an inboard jet pump. Many people consider jet skis as toys, but they are not. The Coast Guard classifies jet skis as Class A inboard boats. Since they are boats, jet skis must be operated in accordance with all the laws and regulations established for boating.

There are a great variety of jet skis. Some jet skis are ridden sitting down. Others can be operated while kneeling or standing up. Some are built for two while others are designed for single riders. Some are even designed to tow waterskiers. There are jet skis designed for quick-turning, tumbling, in-the-water action, while others are designed to keep you dry as you cruise along.

Whatever type you choose, it's a good idea to become familiar with your jet ski. Read the owner's manual and become familiar with all the jet ski features. Have the jet ski dealer show you how all the equipment works.

Where's the Propeller?

Since jet skis are powered by a jet drive, there are no moving parts like a rudder or external propeller. These features make jet skiing safe when the rider falls off.

The jet drive is a simple device. It is composed of an intake, a driveshaft, an impeller (a small internal propeller), and a steering nozzle all contained at the stern in a pump housing within the hull.

Water is drawn through the intake into the pump housing. When it reaches the impeller, the water is pressurized and forced out of the steering nozzle. The steering nozzle directs the jet ski. It is controlled by a handlebar near the front of the jet ski. Even though there is no external propeller to worry

A jet ski doesn't have a propeller—
it's powered by a jet drive!

about, there are some precautions that should be taken:

• Always keep hands, feet, hair, and clothing away from the intake.

• Never attempt to place any objects into the intake.

• Never ride a jet ski in less than two feet of water. Mud or sand can be sucked into the jet drive which may damage it.

Safe Jet Skiing

Before anyone can enjoy the fun and excitement of jet skiing, certain rules and regulations must be followed.

Since they are boats, jet skis must have a Certificate of Number. These numbers are issued by each state. They are used to identify individual boats. Applications for a Certificate of Number can be found at your jet ski dealer.

Don't lose control of your jet ski—
follow all safety rules!

When you get your number, it must be displayed on the forward half of each side of the jet ski. They also must be readable.

Some states have age limits for jet ski operators. Generally, no one under the age of 14 should operate a jet ski. Check the boating laws in your state to find out the age limit.

PFD

A **P**ersonal **F**lotation **D**evice (PFD)—a life-jacket or vest—must be worn at all times when operating a jet ski. There are many kinds of PFDs. Type 1 PFDs are the best and safest. They can turn an unconscious person face up in the water.

Type 2 PFDs can also turn most people face up in the water, but they are not as strong as the Type 1 PFDs. Type 3 PFDs are the most common flotation devices. They offer greater comfort and movement, but they cannot turn an unconscious person face up in the water.

Always wear a PFD (Personal Flotation Device)
when jet skiing.

Before you buy any personal flotation device, make sure it is the right size, and it has the Coast Guard label of approval. This is the only kind of PFD that is legal.

From time to time, it is a good idea to test your PFD. Test it in shallow water and make sure the device keeps your head above the water. Also check the straps, buckles and fasteners so that they are free of rust. And be sure that the fabric of the PFD is not worn or torn. After each use, make sure you let the PFD dry before you store it. This will prevent the fabric from rotting.

It's also a good idea to equip your jet ski with a small fire extinguisher. The extinguisher should also be approved by the Coast Guard.

Before you take to the water, you should know some basic safety rules:

•When overtaking another boat, make sure you keep a safe distance between yourself and the other boat. When someone is overtaking you, allow them to pass before making any turns or maneuvers.

•Always stay to the right when approaching an other boat head-on.

•Stay away from boat channels. If you must cross them, cross them quickly.

•Travel at slower speeds when in a busy area.

•Never operate a jet ski in a swim area.

•Stay away from dams and water falls.

•Don't overload your jet ski. Make sure you do not exceed the established weight limit.

•Never operate a jet ski in a restricted area. Always watch for signs.

•Always be alert and watch for other boats.

•Never operate a jet ski at night.

•Never jet ski in stormy weather.

•Always operate your jet ski at a safe speed (a speed that allows you to avoid collision or to stop).

•When riding in narrow channels, always stay to the right and go slow.

•Stay clear of sailboats. Sailboats always have the right-of-way.

A Jet Ski Check List

It's a good idea to check your jet ski before each outing. This will ensure safety and enjoyment.

•Make sure the steering mechanism works properly.

•Make sure the throttle operates properly.

•Make sure the intake and the jet pump are free of foreign objects.

Keeping your jet ski in good
working order will ensure safety.

•Make sure there are no fuel or oil leaks (to do this, you'll have to remove the seat).

•Make sure all hoses are secure and free of cracks.

•Make sure all water is drained from the engine compartment.

•Make sure you have plenty of fuel.

•Make sure the oil level is proper.

•Make sure the battery is charged.

•Make sure the hull is not damaged.

•Make sure the stop button on the handlebars works properly. Start the engine, let it run, then test the button.

What to Wear?

As with all sports, jet skiing is much more fun—and safer—if you wear the proper gear. A good PFD is a must. You'll also want to wear the proper eye protection. Goggles work the best to protect a rider from the sun, wind, and water spray. Safety glasses also provide protection. For your feet, try deck shoes. They will protect you against scrapes and bruises.

A wet suit is ideal for cooler water and temperatures. It will protect you against hypothermia (abnormally low body temperature) which can paralyze you. Waterproof gloves will protect your hands and provide better gripping power.

Launching Your Jet Ski

If you don't live on a lake, you'll have to use a public launch to gain access to the water. That means you'll have to share the launch with others. Make sure the launch ramp is in good condition. If it's too steep or in poor condition,

A wet suit and gloves will make
jet skiing more enjoyable.

you're better off going to another launch. Also, make sure that the water at the end of the ramp is deep enough for your jet ski.

Starting Out

Jet skis should only be ridden by people who know how to swim. After the jet ski is launched, make sure you start out in at least two feet of water. Stay away from weeds and lily pads. They will clog the intake.

Attach the tether cord on the jet ski to your PFD. Sit or kneel on the jet ski and make sure the way is clear before you start the jet pump. Slowly accelerate by turning the throttle. As soon as you are in open water, you can increase your speed. If you are a beginner, choose an area that is free of boats and swimmers.

Falling

Falling off a boat is no fun. It can also be dangerous. But falling off a jet ski is half the fun—and it will happen. Still, problems and injury can arise if you don't know how to fall off your jet ski properly. When you feel yourself falling, push yourself from the handlebars and roll into the water. The jet ski engine will immediately shut off. (Most jet skis come equipped with an engine shut-off tether that is attached to your PFD. Once you fall, the tether is pulled and shuts off the engine.) Carefully climb back onto the jet ski and restart the engine. Make sure the area is clear before you accelerate.

Jet skiing is lots of fun, but it can get tiring. When you get tired, mistakes can occur. Don't overdo it. When you feel yourself getting tired, take a break.

When you have finished your ride and want to return to shore, make sure the way is clear and that no other boats are leaving the shore. Watch for the no-wake buoys—you can be held respon-

If you know how to fall from a jet ski,
you can avoid injury.

sible for damage to other boats that is caused by your wake. Don't run your jet ski on shore. You may damage the intake. When approaching the shore, shut off the engine, get off the jet ski, and walk it in to shore.

Teaching Others to Jet Ski

Once you become comfortable with jet skiing, you may want to teach others so they can enjoy it too. If you do, make sure others know how to swim, and that they are aware of boating safety rules and regulations. Give them detailed instructions on how the jet ski operates—and make sure the tether is attached to their PFD.

Advanced Riding

Jets skis are highly maneuverable watercraft that can make sharp turns. Before you attempt any advanced riding, make sure you are knowledgeable of your jet ski and the area in which you are riding.

Before you attempt any stunts, make sure
you know your jet ski well.

Find an open stretch of water where there are no other boaters or swimmers. Wave jumping can be exciting—but it also increases the risk of injury. Always be in control of your jet ski, and never attempt a stunt unless you have received the proper training from a responsible advanced rider. Make sure you know the risks involved in each stunt before you attempt one.

Water-skiing

Some jet skis are big and powerful enough to pull a water-skier. If you use your jet skis for water-skiing, make sure you bring a passenger along to watch the skier (this is a law in most states). Anyone being towed on water-skis must wear a PFD.

Check to see if the way is clear. Start at a slow speed until the tow rope tightens. When the skier is ready, apply enough power to raise the skier out of the water. Be responsible when pulling a skier. Stay away from the shore and other boats. When the skier is done, have them settle into the water. Then go pick them up. It's a lot safer than flinging them towards the shore. Make sure you pick up the skis and tow rope before heading in.

Jet Ski Magazines

The best way to learn about new equipment, jet ski events, and riding techniques is through the various jet ski magazines. Here are some of the most popular ones:

•*Jet Skier Magazine*—The official publication of the International Jet Ski Boating Association (IJSBA), 1239 E. Warner Ave., Santa Ana, CA 92705.

•*Personal Watercraft Illustrated*—2201 Cherry Ave., Long Beach, CA 90806

•*Water Scooter*—319 Barry Avenue South, Suite 101, Wayzata, MN, 55391.

Jet ski magazines cover all the important races
like the World Jet Ski Finals.

If you're looking for more jet ski information, try the U.S. Coast Guard office, your nearest jet ski dealer, or your local library.

Jet Ski Clubs

Jet ski clubs and organizations are becoming more numerous as more jet skis are sold. Clubs sponsor group rides, safety clinics, water festivals, and other jet ski activities. And joining a club is a great way to meet new people. Ask your local jet ski dealer about clubs in your area.

Jet ski clubs and organizations sponsor
group activities and races.

A Final Word

Cruising about on a jet ski is a fun and exciting way to enjoy the summer. Remember to respect the rights of other boaters, swimmers, and shoreline property owners. Always operate your jet ski in a safe and responsible manner, and you will get the most enjoyment out of your jet skis.

Jet skiing—an exciting way to enjoy the summer!

GLOSSARY

•Buoys—floats that serve as channel markers and show the location of hidden obstacles.

•Driveshaft—part of the jet pump that turns the impeller.

•Hypothermia—a condition caused by exposure to cold water where the body temperature drops to dangerously low levels.

•Impeller—the internal propeller that pressurizes water.

•Intake—part of the jet pump that draws in the water.

•Jet pump—the device that forces water out of a jet ski.

•Personal flotation device (PFD)—a life vest or jacket that keeps a jet skier afloat.

•Personal watercraft—another name for jet skis.

•Pump housing—part of the jet ski that contains the jet pump.

•Steering nozzle—part of the jet pump that steers the jet ski.

•Tether—the chord that attaches to the PFD and shuts off the jet ski when the rider tumbles.